# THE KIMBERLEY

JOURNEY THROUGH AN ANCIENT LAND

NEW
HOLLAND

# THE KIMBERLEY

JOURNEY THROUGH AN ANCIENT LAND

NICK RAINS

# CONTENTS

# THE KIMBERLEY IN PERSPECTIVE

The Kimberley is situated in the far north-west of Western Australia. This spectacular, rugged and unique region is bordered by the Tanami and Great Sandy deserts to the south and the Timor Sea and the Indian Ocean to the north and west respectively. Covering a staggering 421 000 square kilometres, this remote area has only three major roads. Inhabited for over 40 000 years by Aborigines, today the region has a mixed population of a mere 30 000, concentrated in the four main towns of Derby, Broome, Kununurra and Wyndham.

The rugged Kimberley consists of a central plateau dissected by river gorges and flanked by the deeply folded and faulted King Leopold and Durack ranges. The Ord River and the artificial Lake Argyle—at 5672 million cubic metres, Australia's largest body of fresh water—dominate the eastern Kimberley, while the Fitzroy is the main river in the west.

The monsoonal Kimberley has only two seasons—the Wet and the Dry. Rainfall in the arid southern inland areas ranges from 250 to 500 mm per year, while the tropical coastline to the north receives between 800 and 1200 mm. Temperatures in summer peak between 30 and 40°C and in winter between 26 and 34°C.

**HALF-TITLE PAGE:** The east Kimberley's famous Purnululu.
**TITLE PAGE:** Cypress Pools, on Theda station, form a series of still pools connected by short waterfalls.
**PAGES 4–5:** Gantheaume Point, near Broome, boasts colourful, vibrant sandstone shaped by the Indian Ocean.

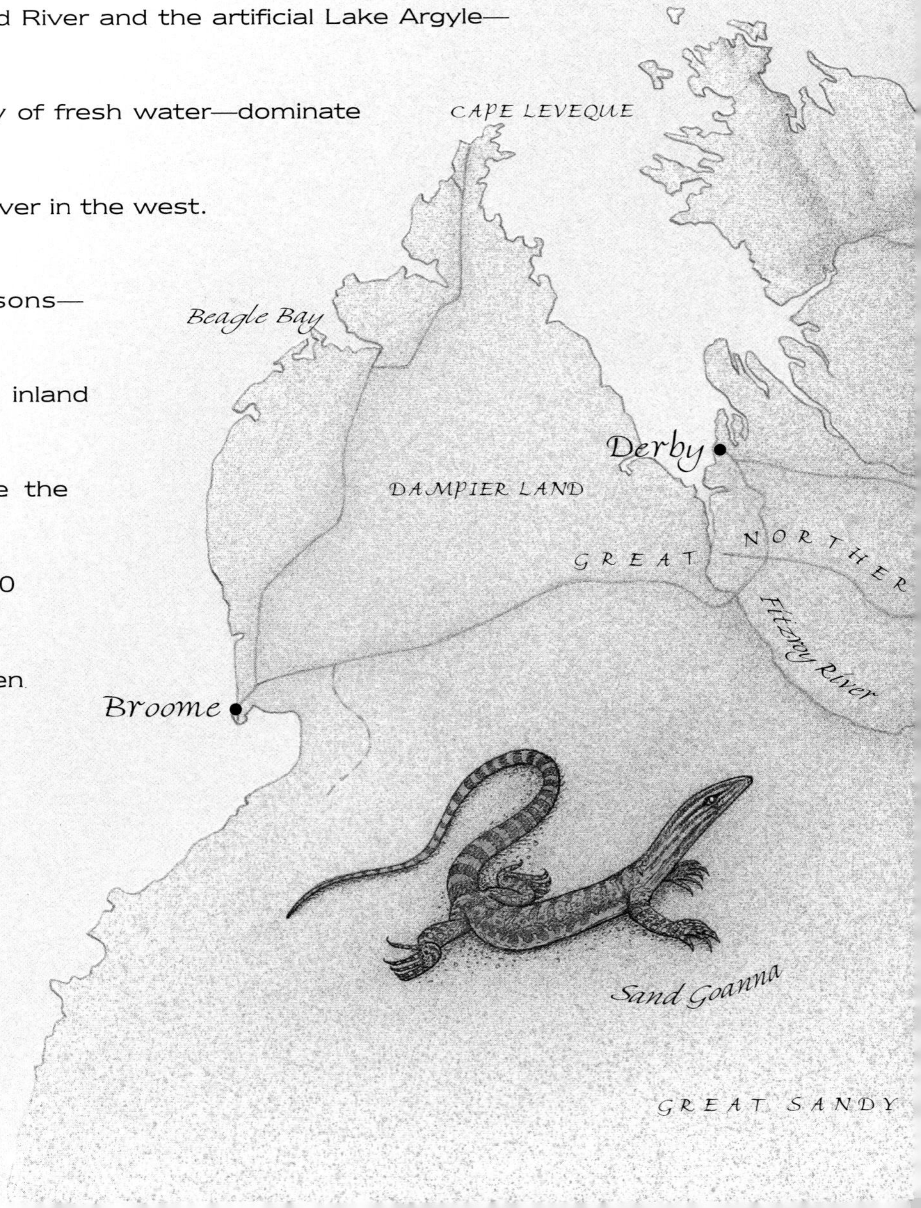

CAPE LEVEQUE

Beagle Bay

Derby

DAMPIER LAND

GREAT NORTHER

Fitzroy River

Broome

Sand Goanna

GREAT SANDY

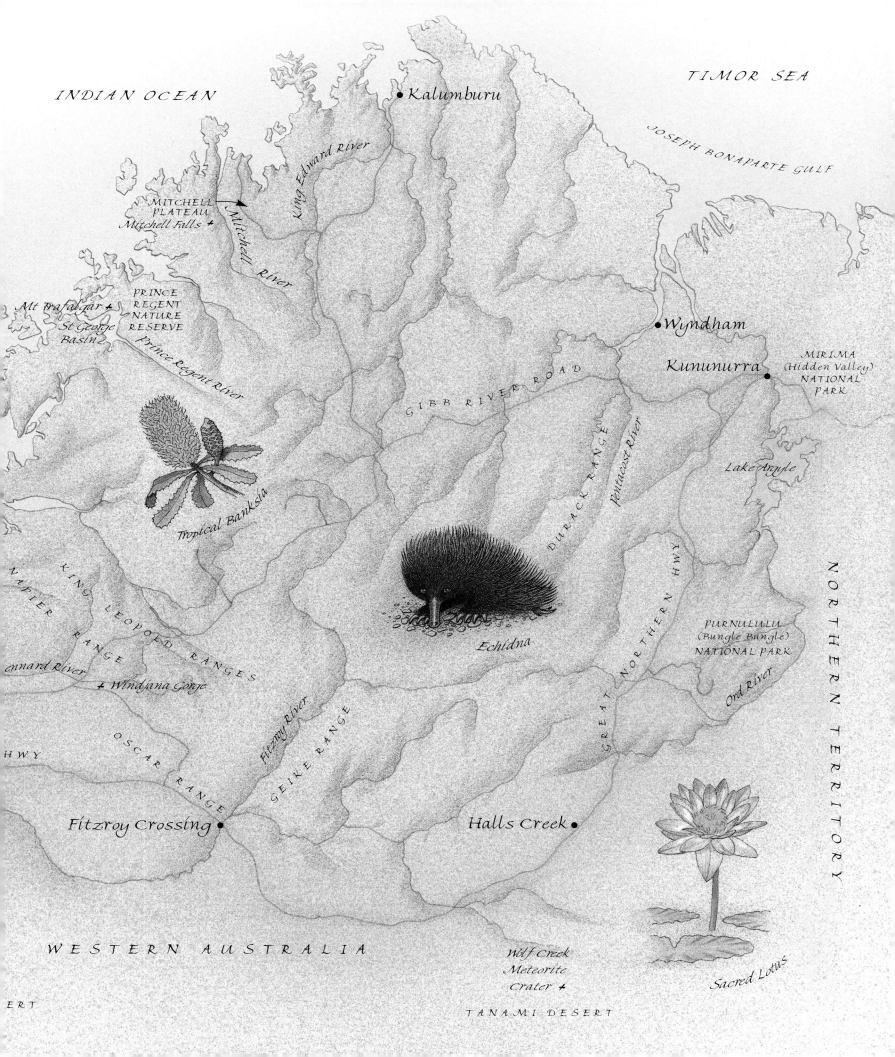

INDIAN OCEAN

TIMOR SEA

JOSEPH BONAPARTE GULF

• Kalumburu

King Edward River

MITCHELL
PLATEAU
Mitchell Falls ✝

Mitchell River

Mt Trafalgar ✝

PRINCE
REGENT
NATURE
RESERVE

St George
Basin

Prince Regent River

• Wyndham

Kununurra

MIRIMA
(Hidden Valley)
NATIONAL
PARK

GIBB RIVER ROAD

DURACK RANGE

Pentacost River

Lake Argyle

Tropical Banksia

NAPIER
RANGE

KING LEOPOLD RANGES

ennard River

✝ Windjana Gorge

Fitzroy River

GEIKE RANGE

OSCAR RANGE

GREAT NORTHERN HWY

NORTHERN TERRITORY

PURNULULU
(Bungle Bungle)
NATIONAL PARK

Ord River

Echidna

HWY

Fitzroy Crossing •

Halls Creek •

WESTERN AUSTRALIA

Wolf Creek
Meteorite
Crater ✝

Sacred Lotus

ERT

TANAMI DESERT

# PREFACE

I spend a lot of time on the road, in the course of my work as a professional photographer, meeting people from families on around-Australia adventures to overseas visitors taking a walk on the wild side. Regardless of the nature of their trip, visitors to the Kimberley region of north-west Australia will tell you how it took hold of their imagination, how they wish they had spent a lot more time there.

I have had the good fortune to visit this remote part of Australia many times in the past eight years, and when I think about it I realise that each time I returned to 'civilisation' I began to plan my next trip back. Before each visit I am almost overwhelmed with anticipation. Since I know the main attractions like the back of my hand, why such excitement?

Could it be the sheer diversity of the region—the incredible range and beauty of the landforms—or the fact that much of the Kimberley is still unknown to non-Aboriginal people and that here one can truly 'get away from it all'? Or maybe it has something to do with the type of people you meet—people who are friendly, helpful and interested in having a chat.

My work takes me into many people's lives, however briefly, and it is important to establish a rapport quickly as my time is often limited. Compared with those in Australia's big cities, I find people in the Kimberley refreshingly open. In the space of half an hour, a conversation with someone you have just met can cover the weather, politics, station life, local gossip and … the weather. I once met an Aboriginal family travelling in the opposite direction on an obscure station track. We pulled up and within five minutes I knew the driver's name, where he had come from, where he was going and why. I knew that his wife had gone to Derby with the Royal Flying Doctor Service and that his kids in the back were on their way to a School of the Air trip. With a parting invitation to visit his station he sped off in a cloud of dust. The Kimberley certainly lives up to the cliché: 'there are no strangers here, just friends you have yet to meet'.

Of course, a large part of what draws me back to the Kimberley time and again is the absolutely awe-inspiring scenery; and that is also what serves as the driving force behind this book. I have attempted to capture some of what it feels like to be there, deep within the most remote area of Australia, thousands of kilometres from any city, possibly hundreds of kilometres from any other person.

What could be better than the utter silence of an outback dawn, the morning light gradually revealing detail and colour in Purnululu's 'beehive' rock formations? The camera only captures a split second on film but watching such a scene evolve in front of my eyes is one of the reasons I enjoy my work so much. Each time I struggle out of sleep at some horrible hour of the morning I find the dawn revealing the landscape in some new way. I am certainly not a morning person by nature; despite this I have yet to see a dawn that doesn't stir me into photographic action, all thoughts of sleep chased away by the rituals of capturing the subtleties of light on film.

Of course, long outback trips are an experience all their own, and the continuous movement becomes a way of life. Weeks seem to fly by and the concerns of the city are far away. Not surprisingly, returning to the 'big smoke', to the speed of modern living and—worst of all—traffic, always comes as a serious jolt.

Not that outback trips themselves are exactly idyllic. Often they can be arduous in many ways, mostly in a physical sense. Gone are the mental pressures of the city and in their place are heat, flies, dust, limited water supplies and isolation. Simple things take on a significance totally out of proportion to what we usually think of as 'normal' life. A long drink of cold water after an exhausting hike in the late afternoon heat becomes a deep pleasure, a shower at the end of a dusty day is indescribably luxurious, and a cool breeze at night can make the difference between a sound sleep and no sleep at all.

I am convinced that discomforts add spice to experience. Many places in this book are not just off the road; they require a bit of a walk to see them. Now, I am not particularly fit—and carrying a heavy pack and tripod makes life even more difficult—but I have found there is a great sense of achievement in exerting yourself in pursuit of fantastic scenery. If it was easy, would it be as worthwhile?

The walk up to Mini Palms Gorge in Purnululu National Park, while only about three kilometres from the car park, is rugged and steep. Yet when you reach the end you are greeted with the incredible sight of a massive gash splitting the rock face—a revelation that makes you forget all thoughts of tiredness and dripping perspiration. I was filled with a new energy as I scrambled around finding good angles from which to shoot, totally absorbed by the feeling of being in this unique spot. Only as I turned for home did I realise how tired I was, but still exhilarated after experiencing such a magnificent place.

*The Kimberley: Journey through an Ancient Land* is a personal look at this wild and marvellous region filled with open-hearted people and adventures wait-

**ABOVE:** My trusty Landcruiser has taken me to some of the most remote parts of Australia—a strong, reliable vehicle is vital when heading off the beaten track. Here we both 'take five' to watch the vivid sunset over the Indian Ocean at Cable Beach near Broome.

ing to be experienced. Other parts of Australia may be just as spectacular but, for me, only the Kimberley completely captures the essence of the Australian outback. Massive waterfalls, quiet billabongs, endless plains and narrow gorges combine to give a true sense of freedom under the tropical blue skies of the remote West Australian north.

*Nicholas Rins*

# THE STORY OF THE KIMBERLEY

The spectacular scenery of the remote Kimberley region in the northern corner of Western Australia attracts visitors from around the country and all over the world. From the famous striped beehive-shaped rock formations of the Purnululu National Park south of Lake Argyle to the mighty cascades of Mitchell Falls in the far north and the sweeping white sands of the beaches that surround Broome, the Kimberley never fails to delight and astound.

Of course, it is not the vast and unique country alone that draws travellers back time and again. The people of the rugged Kimberley have an approach to life that is often found in the more remote parts of outback Australia—hardworking yet easygoing, always ready with a friendly greeting and usually willing to lend a hand when the need arises.

Countless flies and mosquitoes might try to carry you off during the hottest time of the year, but the people who live here believe the Kimberley is the most magnificent place in the country. The land itself is fertile and rich in texture, and the colours are extraordinarily vivid—the blue of the big sky is incredibly deep, sunsets put on a show of magentas and yellows that has to be seen to be believed and the air is as fresh and clean as it gets.

Fresh though the Kimberley may feel, the region is in fact one of the oldest parts of this ancient continent. Some of the rocks in the Lennard Hills and around Bow River in the west have been dated to over two billion years, almost half as old as the earth itself. Unlike ancient rocks in other parts of the world, the rocks of the Kimberley have been subject to little geological activity. While the crumpled Himalayas were formed when two mighty landmasses crunched together, many of the striking features of the modern Kimberley region are the result of water erosion—one of the most powerful forces in nature.

Of these, the most famous would have to be the black-and-orange striped beehives of the Purnululu (Bungle Bungle) National Park. Here the 'cement', which normally fills the gaps between particles in the sandstone, has been washed away. While this leaves the rock vulnerable to even light knocks, it remains immensely strong when compressed. Millions of years of rainwater were therefore able to carve deep canyons in the porous rock while the compressed mounds in between have remained stable. The distinctive striped surface is in fact less than a centimetre thick—a thin protective skin covering soft white sandstone underneath. The orange is made up of clay and silica and the black is organic material. This protective coat is nevertheless extremely fragile and breaking off even a small piece can result in extensive erosion of the sandstone underneath.

**OPPOSITE:** The massive walls of Mini Palms Gorge in Purnululu National Park north-east of Halls Creek dwarf a visitor wandering through the palms. This huge gash in the escarpment recedes into the darkness until it becomes a deep cave which can be explored further with the help of a reliable torch.

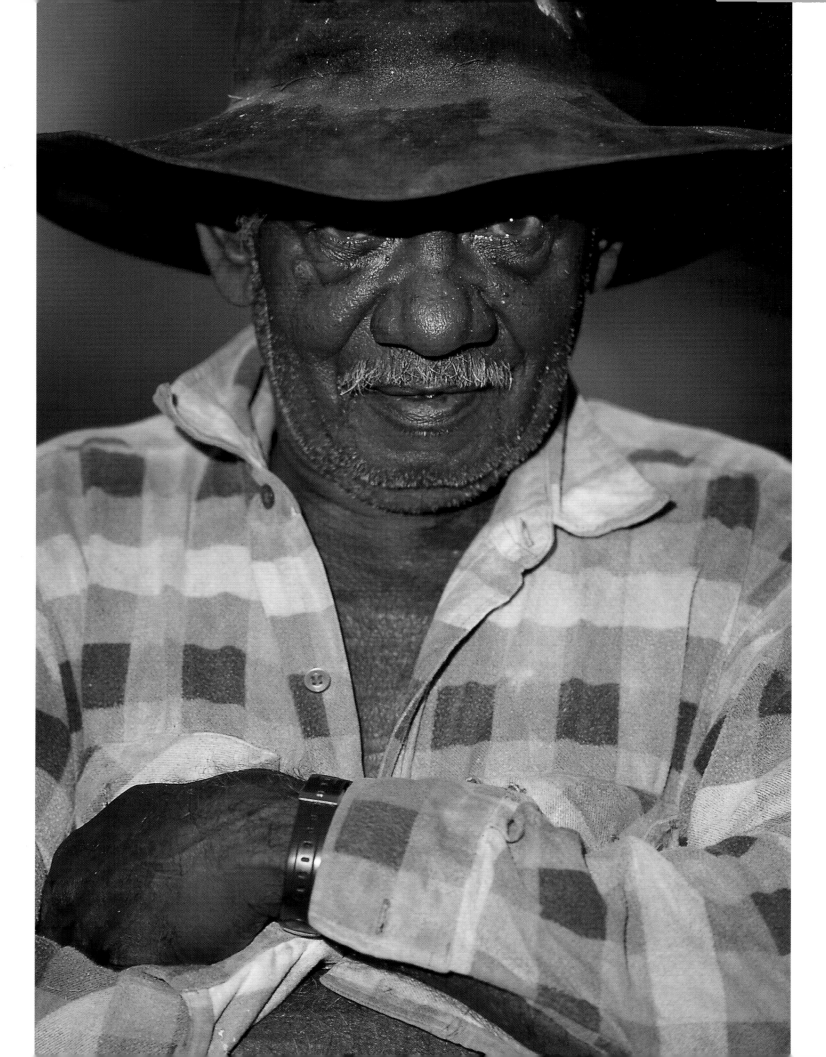

Not least among the fascinating features of the Kimberley are the area's fossil reefs. Around 400 million years ago the region lay deep within the tropics and many of the lower areas were submerged. During this time a coral reef to rival the modern Great Barrier Reef grew around what is the Mitchell Plateau today. The Oscar and Napier ranges to the south are soft limestone remnants of this ancient structure. As the mighty Lennard and Fitzroy rivers sliced through these ranges they sculpted the magnificent Windjana and Geikie gorges—two of the most spectacular gorges in the Kimberley, with soaring limestone walls, permanent water and abundant wildlife.

The lives of those in the Kimberley today are still dominated by water, both its absence and its dramatic presence. While local Aboriginal people recognise seven seasons, the monsoonal climate of the Kimberley can be divided into two: the Wet, from around October to March, and the Dry, from April to the beginning of the Wet. November and December are very unpredictable with high humidity and short local storms occurring most afternoons. January to March is the wettest, hottest and most uncomfortable period as daytime temperatures soar over 40°C and quiet waterholes become raging torrents. The dry season tends to be cool at night with temperatures rarely falling below 35°C during the day.

Nevertheless, because of its enormous area, there is considerable variation in weather across the Kimberley. The Mitchell Plateau can be quite cold in the middle of the Dry and it experiences the most rainfall in the Wet, while Fitzroy Crossing receives considerably less rain and temperatures can fall to nearly

freezing in August. The coastal towns tend to miss the extremes: Broome and the surrounding area are warm year-round and avoid the worst of the scorching temperatures of Fitzroy Crossing in the Wet.

Though huge, the Kimberley is very isolated and has a population of only about 30 000 people, most of whom live in Broome, Kununurra, Derby or Wyndham. The rest live on the many vast pastoral properties scattered around the region. These are generally men and women of few words—the stockmen and station managers tend to fit the image of the strong, silent types of movie westerns. Hard-working people, they have no time for 'slackers' or 'bludgers', but when their respect is earned they will be the best of mates.

The pace of life is not slow, neither is it governed by the clock. When a job needs doing it will be done now, not later, but try to make an appointment with someone and the response is likely to be 'try me on Thursday arvo' or 'sometime in the morning, maybe'. For the people of the Kimberley, priorities are slightly different here—if somebody is late, something probably cropped up which was seen to be more important at the time. It is also quite a challenge to estimate travelling times over such long distances. With a few hundred kilometres to cover, it is very difficult to know what the road conditions will be—and if you are half a day late, well, never mind.

Colonisation in the area can be traced back over 40 000 years, though details of early settlement are sketchy. Modern Aboriginal people are believed to be descended from groups of migrants who travelled along the Malay Peninsula to Java, Bali and thence to the north coast of Australia. The low sea levels at the

OPPOSITE: Many Aboriginal people of the Kimberley work as stockmen, and some of the smaller communities are associated with one particular property. Here, at Mount Elizabeth station, Alex has just finished a long day in the saddle mustering wild cattle in thick bush not far from the homestead.

time made sea crossings easier and it is possible that this was the world's first major migration by sea.

Descendants of the original groups are thought to have spread across the continent over thousands of years. Aboriginal artefacts found on sites along the Ord River date back to over 20 000 years. However, the first areas of settlement would have been on what is today's seabed, since the coast at that time was up to 250 kilometres off the present shoreline.

Aboriginal rock art is one of the few permanent records of the early inhabitants of the Kimberley and the two best-known styles are the Wandjina figures and the Kimberley Dynamic or Bradshaw figures.

The local people believe that the Wandjina figures were painted by the creator beings that now exist in the paintings, trees and landscapes. These beings originated from the north-west with the annual monsoons and could take the form of humans or clouds. When they died, they left a shadow on the wall of their caves and other Wandjinas painted over them, leaving the images we see today. Tribal elders also painted over the figures, maintaining the continuity with the past and reaffirming spiritual connections.

The Bradshaw paintings differ from all other forms of Aboriginal rock art, with the possible exception of the Mimi figures of the Northern Territory. They vary greatly in size and form, but the best known are the Tassled Dynamics which look very much like dancers with tassled decorations on headdresses, waists and arms. It has been speculated that they predate other Australian Aboriginal art and, at possibly 50 000 years old, they could be the oldest form of art on the planet. Locals dismiss the paintings as 'rubbish art' and

say simply, 'not ours', so the origins of these striking figures remain a mystery.

The lifestyle of the Australian Aboriginal people probably changed very little until first contact with Europeans in the 17th century. Dutch mariner Dirk Hartog is credited with being the first European to sight this land. In 1616 he spotted the West Australian coastline but it wasn't until another Dutchman, Abel Tasman, arrived in 1644 that the area was explored. A surviving chart from this expedition maps today's coastline from Cape York to the North West Cape of Western Australia. Many of the contemporary names along the Kimberley coastline originated from this expedition, and from Englishman William Dampier's detailed exploration of the Kimberley coast 44 years later. Within 50 years of first contact, and the introduction of European diseases, the region's original Aboriginal population of around 10 000 had been reduced by half.

The next century saw little more European exploration until Phillip Parker King charted the coastline between 1818 and 1822, braving the extreme tides of the region and heralding a period of intense exploration of the Kimberley coast and mainland. In 1838, Lieutenant George Grey, sponsored by the Royal Geographical Society, set up the first small camps in Hanover Bay at the mouth of the Prince Regent River. Livestock and tropical crops were brought in from Timor to see how the land responded to farming. Grey saw the region's fertility but was not able to raise financial backing from England to colonise the area further. Today, the richness and fertility of the land enables crops like sorghum and lucerne, grown in

OPPOSITE: Yellow dust swirls as well mounted stockmen move a mob of around 1500 cattle to the yards on Carlton Hill station north-west of Kununurra in the eastern Kimberley. Much larger mobs of cattle can be mustered on these wide plains than in the more difficult country of the central Kimberley.

areas such as Beverley Springs, to grow up to 30 centimetres per week in the growing season.

It was not until Alexander Forrest, the West Australian Surveyor-General, visited the area in 1870 that the Kimberley's value as good farming land was realised in other parts of the country. New grazing land became sought after by the pastoralists further south. Soon after Forrest's enthusiastic reports were published cartels applied for land en masse and the Kimberley Pastoral Company, of which Forrest was a member, took over huge areas of the Fitzroy River frontages. While there was little friction initially between local Aborigines and Europeans, when Forrest led the settlement of the Ord and Fitzroy rivers minor clashes became quite frequent.

Around about the same time there was a surge in interest by explorers and prospectors—the West Australian Government had offered a prize of 5000 pounds to the first prospectors to strike workable gold. It was not until 1885, however, that local prospectors Hall and Slattery went public with their finds around Halls Creek. After word got out on the bush telegraph, gold fever hit and by 1886 more than 2000 prospectors were scattered around the area, leading to further clashes with the local population. Conditions were very harsh and only a few early miners, and the local storekeepers, made any money at all and by 1887 the population was under 500.

Landowners in the east were still determined to utilise the fertile land of the far north-west. They soon took matters into their own hands and began a series of colossal cattle drives with the aim of establishing huge cattle properties in the Kimberley's seemingly limitless grasslands. In 1883 some of the most famous names in the cattle business, including Donald MacDonald and 'Patsy' Durack, started the first of the long cattle drives.

It took the Duracks nearly three years to move their stock from Thylungra station in eastern Queensland to what is now Argyle Downs near Purnululu National Park. In the world's longest-ever cattle drive, pastoralist Donald MacDonald drove 670 head of cattle more than 5000 kilometres from the Goulburn area in New South Wales to an area near Fitzroy Crossing to set up Fossil Downs. These pastoralists were giants of their time, establishing the Kimberley as the country's major cattle-producing region and contributing to the immense wealth of Western Australia's natural resources—minerals such as iron ore and gold.

Today, the cattle stations that make up the bulk of the Kimberley Region are vast—even by Australian standards—making beef one of the major industries in the Kimberley. Many stations comprise over 110 000 hectares, supporting over 40 000 head of cattle; and homesteads are usually 100 kilometres or more from their immediate neighbours.

The Kimberley's distance from Australia's major cities puts economic pressure on the many cattle stations as exports and supplies of even basic goods are subject to huge freight costs. The region is so far from Western Australia's capital city of Perth—over 3000 kilometres to the south—that it identifies more closely with Darwin in the Northern Territory. Station hands are more likely to travel there for a bit of a break than take a huge trip down to the State capital.

OPPOSITE: Douglas takes a shortcut between the different sections of the cattle yards on Carlton Hill station where most of the sorting and branding is done. This is hard and dusty work as each animal must be branded, sorted for size and checked for condition before being moved to the appropriate yard.

Going anywhere during the wet season is usually quite difficult. Most activities on the stations come to a standstill as station tracks are quagmires and main roads are closed to save them from being too badly damaged. Getting around is only possible by air and even then some airstrips may be closed. During this time, many stations release staff and the owners settle down to wait out the Wet, carrying out general maintenance and repairs that have been put off during the hectic pace of the dry season mustering. Life can be pretty lonely on the more remote stations at this time of the year, with just a couple of people staying the whole season and only the occasional mail delivery by plane to break up the week.

Modern communications are a godsend. Most stations have microwave-linked phones, high-frequency radios for the School of the Air, and can pick up the ABC on television. Many stations carry large stocks of food to tide them over if the Wet runs into April or even May if there is late, heavy rain.

Tourism is becoming an ever-increasing part of the Dry as this is the best time for visitors—the earlier the better since the rivers will still be flowing and the countryside will be green and lush from the Wet. In the Kimberley, there are no five-star hotels, no taxis, casinos or poolside bars. Instead, visitors can expect spectacular rocky mountains, superb gorges, unspoiled beaches and peaceful waterholes. The isolation and lack of creature comforts adds to the whole experience; there is a huge sense of satisfaction to be had from simple pleasures like swimming in the cool water of Bell Creek after a very hot half-hour walk. The tourist season starts in earnest in May, and there are visitors from all over Australia and the world right through until late October, the end of the Dry.

Travellers can explore the Kimberley by taking one of the three major roads that cover the area: the sealed Great Northern Highway, connecting the towns of Kununurra and Broome; the unsealed but fairly well-maintained Gibb River Road, also connecting Kununurra and Broome; and the Kalumburu Road, which links the Gibb River Road with Kalumburu, a small Aboriginal settlement on the north coast. Apart from the Great Northern Highway, all roads are dirt and are very demanding on vehicles, so it is best to travel by four-wheel-drive. Some tour operators in the region use commercial four-wheel-drive buses, while others use regular four-wheel-drive wagons such as the Toyota Landcruiser.

Travelling by air is another way to get around the area—the Ibis Aerial Highway links many places—and most stations have an all-weather airstrip. For people with limited time this is an excellent option as it allows easy access to the most remote areas. Between May and September many stations open their doors to visitors who would like to find out more about life on a cattle station.

Mount Elizabeth, Beverley Springs, Drysdale and Theda stations, to mention just a few, offer a range of accommodation, from basic campsites to cabins. Visitors can watch normal station activities such as yardwork, branding and horse breaking, and station owners will often point the way to little-known spots—a delightful, secluded waterhole or a rare rock-art site. Activities such as bushwalking and birdwatching have also become extremely popular in

**OPPOSITE:** A solitary boab tree stands silhouetted against a cloudless Kimberley sunset, its distinctive bulbous trunk in stark contrast to its stubby limbs and delicate leaves. The boab, a relative of the African baobab, is almost an icon of the Kimberley, although it is also found across the border in the Northern Territory.

the region, with some stations such as Theda catering specifically to natural history groups.

The Kimberley Region is a natural-history lover's paradise. Plant life in the area is nothing short of spectacular. More than 2000 plant species have been described in the region, and many more have yet to be named. Many of the plants play an important part in local Aboriginal culture—either as food, raw materials or as indicators of seasonal changes. Bush tucker is also becoming quite popular in the city and many local communities supply plants which are exclusive to the region to interstate gourmet restaurants. Local Aboriginal health services have also stimulated a great deal of interest in traditional bush medicines.

Two of the most striking trees on the Australian continent are found in the Kimberley—the boab and the Mitchell Fan Palm. The boab could easily be the symbol of the region. Huge and expressive, these trees take on an enormous variety of shapes, the trunks ranging from gnarled, twisted nightmares to smooth, sleek wine bottles. Boabs are quick-growing and can live for over 1000 years, mature trees sometimes reaching a height and width of 25 metres.

Boab trees were of great importance to the local Aborigines. The seeds are high in protein and the pulp contains various important supplements including ascorbic acid and malic. Water can be extracted from large cavities in the trunk, the tree gum can be used as glue and the bark can be used to make string. During the Dry, the leaves are shed to conserve water and the resultant bare skeleton standing stark against a vivid magenta sunset is one of the Kimberley's most memorable sights.

The equally distinctive Mitchell Fan Palm, part of the Livistonia family, is found in large numbers on the Mitchell Plateau. The trees can reach 18 metres in height, with the fan-shaped leaves forming a crown at the top of the smooth trunk, the leaf stalks often 2 metres long. Aboriginal people use the growing shoots as an important source of food. They can be eaten raw or cooked, but removing them tends to kill the palms, which are fairly slow-growing.

The Kimberley is also a fabulous place for bird-watchers—even those who are not particularly interested in the subject find themselves frequently reaching for a copy of a field guide. Birds of all kinds can be seen throughout the year, especially at the beginning of the dry season when the billabongs are full and the grass is at its greenest.

Marlgu Billabong, north-west of Kununurra, is an excellent birdwatching area. Visitors are encouraged to take the fine walkway out to a delightful bird hide, and sitting in the shade with a pair of good binoculars is a magnificent way to start the day. It should be easy to spot jacanas or Jesus birds, black cockatoos, whistling kites, brolgas, rainbow bee-eaters, azure kingfishers and the occasional jabiru or red-legged stork. Some birds migrate from as far away as Siberia; some pass through, heading further south; and some will nest in the Kimberley, raise their young and then return to their country of origin.

Of course, water is a major attraction for birds. One of the Purnululu National Park campgrounds offers visitors to the area a continuously flowing 'bush shower' surrounded by tiny darting birds. Finches, wrens and honeyeaters regard the intruder as a

OPPOSITE: Waterholes that are well inland are usually considered safe from the powerful saltwater crocodile—the most infamous inhabitant of northern Australia. These inland waters are more commonly the home of the freshwater crocodile (*Crocodylus johnstonii*), seen here in Windjana Gorge.

minor nuisance and get on with the business of drinking from puddles. Standing in clear cold water on a hot day identifying at least a dozen different bird species within metres is a truly unique experience.

Of all the wildlife in the Kimberley, birds are the easiest to spot; but there many other animals exclusive to the country, most of which are difficult to see without a bit of patience. Crocodiles are obvious, if you know where to look. The large and extremely dangerous saltwater crocodile inhabits the mangrove-fringed coast, but they can also be found far upstream in the rivers. Generally, waterfalls prevent them from moving too far inland, but it is always wise to check with the locals before swimming.

Freshwater crocodiles are much more reclusive than their bigger, fiercer cousins. They grow up to 3 metres in length and inhabit freshwater billabongs and rivers. Most people are likely to see only a large splash and a swirl of water as these animals are very shy. Again, patience is a virtue, and spending a quiet hour by a rocky waterhole will often get results. The best place to see 'freshies' is at Windjana Gorge where the resident crocs are used to visitors and, rather than disappearing at the slightest movement, they will glide off gently in order to keep their distance. At night, a torch will reveal dozens of pairs of reflective eyes in the blackness of the pools.

Crocodiles are only two of the many reptile species found in the Kimberley. Goannas are quite common, very shy, and sometimes fairly large—the spectacular Gould's goanna grows to around 2 metres. Visitors might also come across numerous monitor and legless lizards, skinks and many species of dragon lizard, the most famous being the frilled lizard. Some fire warning signs at the side of the road read: 'We like our lizards frilled not grilled!'

Snakes are also common in the area and will generally slide off well before being spotted. While they should be considered extremely dangerous—treat all snakes with caution—like most animals they would rather avoid a confrontation. Just to be safe, however, carry pressure bandages at all times—a cornered snake can be lethal. The most common snakes in the area are the northern death adder, the western brown and the black whip snake.

Mammals are not as easily spotted as birds and reptiles since many of them, like the yellow-lipped bat, are nocturnal. However, lucky visitors might come across some of Australia's unique range of marsupials, perhaps the scaly-tailed possum or the monjon, a wallaby. Kangaroos are not as common in the Kimberley as in other parts of Australia; mostly it is wallabies that will be seen, but the occasional 'big red' may be glimpsed at the edges of the deserts around Fitzroy Crossing or Halls Creek.

Unique in so many ways, the unspoiled Kimberley may be remote but it is that quality that makes it so exciting. From the Wolf Creek Meteorite Crater on the edge of the Tanami Desert to the dinosaur footprints off Gantheaume Point near Broome, the region is just waiting to be explored. *The Kimberley: Journey through an Ancient Land* is an introduction to the many delights that await those willing to venture into this vast and rugged landscape of towering gorges, tumbled red-rock escarpments, abundant wildlife, quiet, deep waterholes and pristine beaches.

**OPPOSITE:** Normal vehicles can travel along the remote Gibb River Road—most of its 640 kilometres is fairly well maintained—but only a good four-wheel-drive will allow travellers to deal safely with the unexpected ruts, potholes and washouts that are often encountered on outback roads and tracks.

# GIBB RIVER ROAD

# GATEWAY TO GORGE COUNTRY

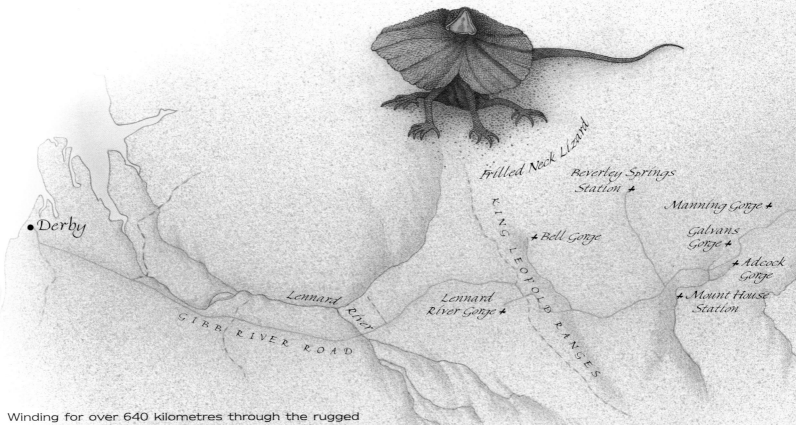

Frilled Neck Lizard

Derby

Beverley Springs
Station

Manning Gorge

Bell Gorge

Galvans
Gorge

Adcock
Gorge

Lennard River

Lennard
River Gorge

Mount House
Station

GIBB RIVER ROAD

KING LEOPOLD RANGES

Winding for over 640 kilometres through the rugged heart of the spectacular Kimberley region, the Gibb River Road allows access to some of the area's most magnificent scenery. Sometimes called the 'Beef Road', it was originally constructed to facilitate the movement of cattle from isolated pastoral properties deep in the tumbled ranges of the central Kimberley.

Twenty years ago it was just a track from Derby to Kununurra via the Gibb River cattle station. Although shorter than the Great Northern Highway route by over 200 kilometres, it was very hard on vehicles and the journey took two or three days. Since then the road has been widened and upgraded and, while still

**PREVIOUS PAGES:** The delightful pool below the falls at popular Bell Gorge offers safe swimming in crystal-clear water while a shady ledge by the water's edge provides protection from the intense Kimberley sun.

unsealed and vulnerable to closure during the Wet, it is now just about negotiable by ordinary cars.

Soon after leaving Derby, the road traverses endless plains dotted with the Kimberley's bulbous-trunked boab trees, but the real adventure begins between Lennard River and Mount House station. Here the road passes through 'Gorge Country' where some of the Kimberley's spectacular and most accessible waterholes and gorges—such as Lennard, Manning and Bell—are to be found.

The Lennard River cuts through the mighty King Leopold Ranges at Lennard Gorge where a short but steep walk into the dramatic narrow slot canyon leads to a delightful deep plunge pool. The access trail off the main road is short but heavily eroded and requires a high clearance four-wheel-drive.

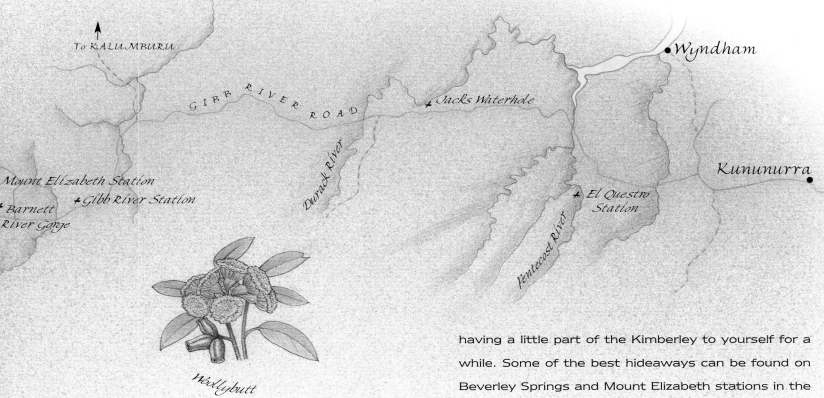

To KALUMBURU

GIBB RIVER ROAD

Durack River

Jack's Waterhole

Wyndham

Kununurra

El Questro Station

Pentecost River

Mount Elizabeth Station

Gibb River Station

Barnett River Gorge

*Woollybutt*

Bell Gorge, a little further down a track off the main road, is simply stunning. Just half an hour's walk from the carpark, the gorge offers safe swimming under the falls and gives visitors the opportunity to view the vivid red cliffs all around. A whole day can easily be whiled away here—exploring the tumbled rocks, swimming in the cool pools and relaxing in the shade.

Many other beautiful gorges lie along the length of the Gibb River Road: the peaceful Adcock and Galvans, only short distances from the road with quiet pools and rocky amphitheatres; Manning Gorge, more of a waterhole, and a tranquil spot to spend a hot day; and Upper Manning and Barnett River gorges, both of which require a trek in of several kilometres.

The more adventurous might like to seek out remote spots on cattle stations in the area. These require a fair amount of effort and a four-wheel-drive to get to, but the reward is the exquisite pleasure of having a little part of the Kimberley to yourself for a while. Some of the best hideaways can be found on Beverley Springs and Mount Elizabeth stations in the central Kimberley and on El Questro near the Kununurra end of the road. El Questro has, for many years, catered for both self-sufficient travellers and those with a taste for the good life.

All stations provide fine camping grounds for visitors. Each extends over 250 000 hectares and some areas are so vast and inaccessible they have not been fully explored even by the owners.

Past the turnoff to Kalumburu and the far north, the heavily folded ranges of the south-west give way to broad plains and rolling hills. Jack's Waterhole on the Durack River, with its general store and billabong campsite, is an excellent spot to break the journey before the final hurdle of the Pentecost River crossing. The river is tidal at this point and the rocky ford can be impassable even during the dry season. From here it is just 60 kilometres to the start of the sealed Great Northern Highway and the Kununurra end of the Gibb River Road.

**ABOVE:** Along the track to Lennard Gorge the road deteriorates markedly and the last kilometre or so requires four-wheel-drive in earnest. **OPPOSITE:** At Lennard Gorge the Lennard River drops 20 metres into a deep cold pool before rushing through a narrow slot canyon only 3 metres wide; it is possible to swim and scramble into the depths of the gorge when the water is low. A pair of harmless water monitor lizards live in the main pool and have surprised many a swimmer as they glide past.

RIGHT: Below the main cascade in Bell Gorge the creek tumbles over a series of smaller waterfalls before finally dropping 20 metres into another large pool. Few people venture this far—the way down is more a scramble than a walk—so it is quite common to have this delightful place all to yourself.

**ABOVE:** Stockhorses in the Kimberley are usually turned out into the stations' vast paddocks to fend for themselves during the wet season. Before mustering starts again early in the Dry these horses must be rounded up and rebroken. Here on Mount House station a young stockman takes time to calm his recently mustered mount before attempting to put on a saddle.

**ABOVE:** In trackless bush elsewhere in Australia, modified four-wheel-drives and motorcycles are often used for mustering but most of the Kimberley region is too rough and rocky to use such vehicles safely—in this remote corner of Australia horses are still the preferred option. Here a group of stock-men move a small mob of cattle to the yards on Mount House station after an early season muster.

ABOVE: Smooth-barked gum trees in Adcock Gorge shine in the soft light of a late dry season rain shower. OPPOSITE: For most of the year Adcock Gorge—just off the Gibb River Road in the central Kimberley—is a peaceful spot for a night's camp and a cool swim. It is hard to believe these tranquil pools become swirling cauldrons when the wet season starts in earnest.

ABOVE: An approaching storm threatens camp on the Charnley River about 80 kilometres from Beverley Springs station in the western Kimberley. Late in the dry season, severe afternoon storms like this one spring up incredibly quickly but tend to pass over just as suddenly.

**ABOVE:** Lovely Lower Manning Gorge, halfway along the Gibb River Road between Kununurra and Broome, provides a cool place to relax and unwind after a long dusty day on the road. The waterhole is safe for swimming, and floating about on an airbed is a great way to spend the hottest part of the day.

**ABOVE:** On Mount Elizabeth station in the centre of the Kimberley the country is so rugged that wild cattle are still mustered on horseback. Each stockman uses 2 or 3 horses in rotation and, as good horses are vital, most are bred and trained by the stockmen themselves. **OPPOSITE:** De-horning is a dangerous but essential part of the muster as sharp tips can easily injure horses, riders or other cattle. **FOLLOWING PAGES:** In the Wet this main crossing over the Pentecost River south-west of Wyndham is covered by a raging torrent and, even in the Dry, a high tide can put a metre of water over the ford.

# MITCHELL PLATEAU

# THE RUGGED NORTH

A visit to any part of the Kimberley is an adventure, but those seeking an experience right off the beaten track tend to head north towards the magnificent waterfalls and gorges of the Mitchell Plateau and the Aboriginal community of Kalumburu, on the edge of the Timor Sea. Here the cattle stations are bigger, the landscape increasingly rugged and the isolation almost palpable. This area is also home to some spectacular examples of Aboriginal rock art.

The track north leaves the Gibb River Road in the heart of the Kimberley and, as it winds up into the plateau region, the landscape gradually changes. Flat grasslands give way to more rugged terrain, and stands of Mitchell Fan Palms, exclusive to the Kimberley, indicate a higher altitude and a slightly cooler, wetter climate. Four-wheel-drive vehicles are recommended, as the Wet closes the road from early January until as late as April or May.

The distance from the turnoff to Kalumburu on the edge of the Timor Sea is 255 kilometres and the only place outside the community to stock up on fuel is Drysdale station, 60 kilometres north of the Gibb River Road. This is also the place to get advice on the condition of the road up onto the Mitchell Plateau.

The Mitchell Plateau and Mitchell Falls are on most visitors' must-see list—and with good reason. The magnificent falls are easily the largest in the Kimberley Region and the journey in is arduous enough to make the experience worthwhile. Not long ago, the 85-kilometre trip from the Kalumburu road to

PREVIOUS PAGES: Some striking Kimberley Dynamic (or Bradshaw) figures are found in the King Edward River region. Unusual amongst Aboriginal rock art, these ancient paintings have not been retouched by later artists.

the falls' camping area took at least three hours. A new road has recently been built which should help travellers avoid the worst of the swampy areas.

Some of the best campsites in the Kimberley lie downstream of the King Edward River crossing, about 10 kilometres along the Mitchell Plateau road. Good, clean drinking water, safe swimming, excellent fishing and superb Aboriginal rock art sites make this a fabulous spot to spend a couple of days.

The Mitchell Falls themselves are spectacular—a series of four cascades where the Mitchell River drops off the plateau on its way to the sea. Sheets of water slip across flat slabs of rock before finally plummeting into the huge pool below. The best way to see the falls is by helicopter and two are stationed right at the campground during the Dry.

An overflight is also the best way to see some of the spectacular scenery of the Prince Regent Nature Reserve just to the south. The mighty Mount Trafalgar presides over the St George Basin at the mouth of the Prince Regent River, and the river itself is an incredible sight from the air, running dead straight for 100 kilometres.

Past the turnoff to the Mitchell Plateau, Theda station has recently opened its doors to visitors. Tracks have been marked to pristine waterholes such as the isolated Honeymoon Pools and Cypress Pool.

At the end of the road, on the banks of the King Edward River, lies the small community of Kalumburu, the old mission buildings and orchards evidence of past religious fervour. A permit is required to visit this area, and accommodation must be organised in advance. The coast offers excellent fishing; ask around in the community and someone will let you know where they are biting that day.

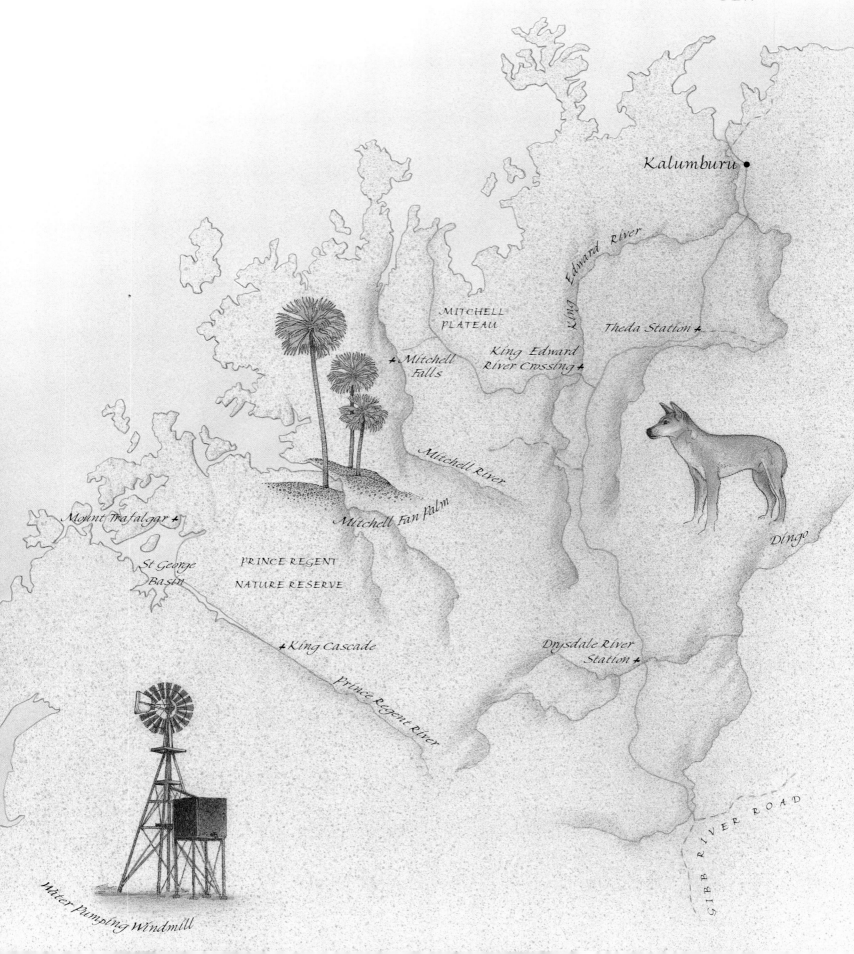

TIMOR SEA

Kalumburu •

King Edward River

MITCHELL PLATEAU

Theda Station +

King Edward River Crossing +

+ Mitchell Falls

Mitchell River

Mount Trafalgar +

Mitchell Fan Palm

Dingo

St George Basin

PRINCE REGENT NATURE RESERVE

Drysdale River Station +

+ King Cascade

Prince Regent River

GIBB RIVER ROAD

Water Pumping Windmill

RIGHT: The staring other-worldly faces of the Kimberley's Wandjina figures, such as these near the King Edward River in the far north, are most often found across the centre of the region. Many of the best examples have been painted under rock ledges that are close to permanent water.

**ABOVE:** In the fading light of dusk the King Edward River tumbles over a rocky ledge on the way to meet the sea near Kalumburu in the far north. Not far from the Mitchell Falls track and with superb campsites nearby, this spot is a good place to spend the night before tackling the trek to the falls.

**ABOVE:** Mark Timms of Theda station in the Kimberley's far north drives three passengers deep into remote parts of the property in his beaten up Suzuki jeep. This ancient knockabout vehicle has been used to rescue surprised 'city slickers' bogged in brand new four-wheel-drives on their way to the sometimes inaccessible King Edward Falls on the King Edward River. **OPPOSITE:** Dogs are often an integral part of station life and 'Jim' goes everywhere with his owner, Mark Timms.

**ABOVE:** Honeymoon Pools is just one of the many wonderful spots scattered across Theda station's 140 000 hectares. Visits to this delightful area are limited to one group at a time in order to minimise human impact on the environment and to keep the area as pristine as possible into the future.

**ABOVE:** Kimberley Heath (*Calytrix exstipulata*) creates a pink haze covering the rocky outcrops of the Mitchell Falls area in the far north and is found across the Kimberley region. Known to the Bardi people of the Dampier Land peninsula as 'gidigid', this pretty shrub is sometimes called Turkey Bush or Kimberley Heather. **OPPOSITE:** The glorious cascades of the Mitchell Falls on the Mitchell Plateau produce a mighty rumble which overpowers all other noise. This rocky amphitheatre is a popular destination for travellers.

RIGHT: High above the St George Basin, the sandstone walls of flat-topped Mount Trafalgar glow in the afternoon light. Part of the Prince Regent Nature Reserve, this area is only accessible by boat (a permit is required) or by air—perhaps the best way to appreciate the spectacular scale and grandeur of the region.

**ABOVE:** The only road north off the Gibb River Road ends at the Aboriginal community of Kalumburu where there is excellent fishing off the beaches and among the mangroves. **OPPOSITE:** The remote region around Kings Cascades on the Prince Regent River is spectacular from the air—the river follows an unusually regular fault in the rock and runs straight as an arrow for over 100 kilometres.

# EASTERN KIMBERLEY

# GATEWAY TO PURNULULU

The eastern Kimberley—roughly encompassing the area north of the Tanami Desert to Joseph Bonaparte Gulf and east from the Durack Range to the Northern Territory border—is as fascinating and full of contrasts as any part of this remote and rugged region.

The area around Kununurra, the largest of the Kimberley towns, is dominated by the Ord River and the mighty artificial Lake Argyle—the heart of the only recently successful Ord River irrigation project. Not far from the southern tip of Lake Argyle, gnawing at the base of the Ragged Range, the Argyle Diamond Mine produces over a third of the world's diamonds. To the north and south, vast cattle stations spread across the land, forming an integral part of the Kimberley's beef industry, once the lifeblood of the region. Today, as dusty stockmen toil on horseback, travellers in their four-wheel-drives head for the magnificent beehive-like striped domes of the Purnululu National Park north-east of Halls Creek.

Kununurra was constructed in the early 1960s to service the Ord River irrigation scheme, although recently the Argyle Diamond Mine and a new sugar mill are more responsible for the town's continuing prosperity. It was built in the wide Ord River valley, where huge escarpments of red rock tower over the surrounding flat floodplains.

While beef is still one of the most important industries in the Kimberley, tourism has increased dramatically over the past 10 years and is now a major source of income for the area. Kununurra, like Broome in the west, is a gateway to the Kimberley

and local operators offer fabulous trips to almost all parts of this magnificent region.

Purnululu National Park—situated approximately 300 kilometres to the south, between Lake Argyle and Halls Creek—is one of the most popular destinations. The characteristic orange-and-black-striped domes are truly unique and the ambience of the deep chasms is quite captivating. It is not unusual to find people talking in hushed voices, especially in Cathedral Gorge where the huge amphitheatre at the end magnifies whispers dramatically.

Closer to Kununurra it is possible to take a flying tour to the Argyle Diamond Mine or a scenic flight over Lake Argyle revealing the thousands of islands formed when the valleys were flooded in the early 1970s. While overflights are spectacular, the lake is also only an hour's drive from town and boat trips and fishing charters are available from Lake Argyle Village. Fishing is particularly popular on the lower Ord River where barramundi abound.

**PREVIOUS PAGES:** The amazing striped sandstone mounds of Purnululu National Park are spectacular from the air and overwhelmingly beautiful at ground level.

Fitzroy Crossing

GREAT NORTHERN HWY

The wetlands around Kununurra, home to vast numbers of migrating birds each year, offer marvellous opportunities for birdwatching. The Ord River was dammed just outside Kununurra in 1972, creating a network of lagoons and billabongs known as the Everglades and, further downstream, the river forms a series of wetlands known as Parry's Lagoon. The natural Marlgu Lagoon near Wyndham, to Kununurra's north, has a well-designed hide for particularly keen birdwatchers.

Wildlife is also abundant in Mirima National Park on the outskirts of Kununurra. Early morning visitors to this 'lost city' of rocky towers and deep canyons will often see agile or short-eared rock wallabies as well as echidnas and various species of bats.

With so many fabulous things to see and do in and around Kununurra, visitors find themselves often lingering much longer than intended before heading off into the tumbled wilds of the even more isolated central Kimberley and Fitzroy Crossing.

Jacana

Wyndham
Marlgu Billabong ✦
Carlton Hill Station ✦

✦ Parry's Lagoon

Kununurra
MIRIMA
(Hidden Valley)
NATIONAL PARK
The Everglades ✦

DURACK RANGE

RAGGED RANGE

✦ Argyle Downs
✦ Lake Argyle Village

Lake Argyle

Argyle Diamond Mine ✦

Ord River

GREAT NORTHERN HWY

PURNULULU
(Bungle Bungle)
NATIONAL PARK

Agile Wallaby

Halls Creek ● ✦ China Wall

Brolga

TANAMI DESERT

**ABOVE:** The beef industry has been one of the most important resources of the Kimberley since the late 19th century and Carlton Hill station, running around 40 000 head of cattle, is one of the largest operations in the region. Mustering and yarding such huge numbers of animals takes the whole dry season—hot, hard work twelve hours a day, seven days a week for months on end.

**ABOVE:** Stockmen are a hardy breed. Most are young men 'doing their time', enduring long dusty hours in the saddle before returning to less remote stations in other states as top hands or managers.

**FOLLOWING PAGES:** The view from the mustering helicopter shows stockmen swirling a mob of cattle in a large holding pen to get them used to horsemen before the drive to the main yards.

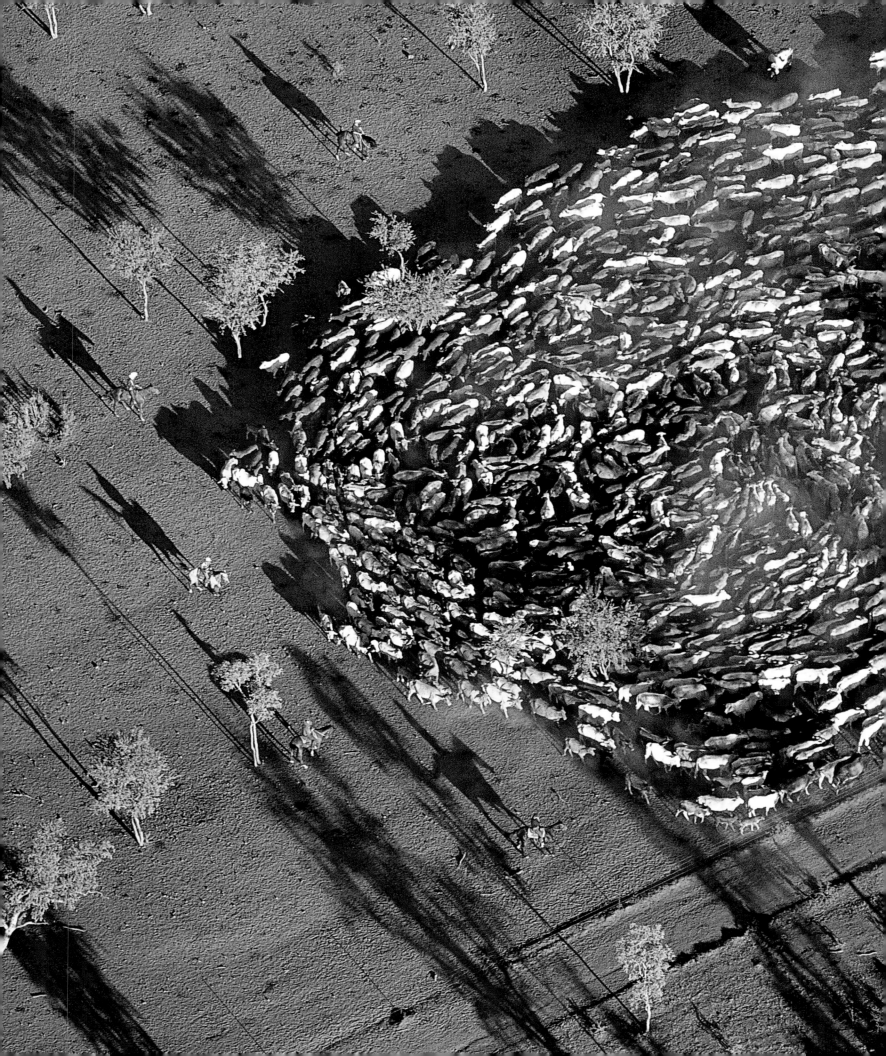

**THESE PAGES:** Once in the main yards of Carlton Hill station, the cattle are checked one by one and split up according to size and condition. The smaller ones will be returned to the paddocks, some will be used for breeding and others will be loaded onto huge road trains and sent to Fremantle for export to countries around the world such as the United States, Indonesia and the Philippines.

**THESE PAGES:** Just outside Kununurra, vast permanent wetlands known as the Everglades—a series of winding billabongs and lagoons created when the diversion dam was built as part of the Ord River irrigation project—attract huge numbers of migratory birds each year from as far away as Siberia. **FOLLOWING PAGES:** The rocks of the Everglades' Sleeping Buddha glow a fiery orange in the last rays of the setting sun.

**THESE PAGES:** The lily-covered Marlgu Billabong forms part of the Parry Lagoons area of natural wetlands north-west of Kununurra. These permanent waterholes are of vital importance to the local ecology—migratory birds visit the lagoons in huge numbers during the Dry, and the Wet sees water-birds such as the jacana **(OPPOSITE BOTTOM)** revel in the abundance of food during the breeding season.

**ABOVE:** Late evening light makes these golden tussocks of spinifex appear deceptively soft. One of the most common grasses in northern Australia, its needle-like leaves can pierce denim, making it very unpopular with bushwalkers. **OPPOSITE:** Within the town limits of Kununurra a labyrinth of narrow red-rock canyons and dead-end gorges forms little Mirima National Park, once aptly known as Hidden Valley. Keen eyes might spot Aboriginal paintings and artefacts in the more remote corners of the park.

**LEFT:** Spectacular Lake Argyle, south of Kununurra, was created in 1972 as part of the Ord River irrigation project. Covering around 740 square kilometres with hundreds of bays and inlets to explore, it is the largest artificial lake in Australia.

**FOLLOWING PAGES:** The narrow chasm of Cathedral Gorge in Purnululu National Park opens into a huge amphitheatre with red-rock walls towering over a perfectly still pool.

**ABOVE:** Aptly named the China Wall, this striking rock formation near Halls Creek is the result of a hard vein of quartz weathering more slowly than the material around it. Other remnants of the 'wall' can be seen winding over nearby hills. **OPPOSITE:** An aerial view of the beehive domes of Purnululu highlights the black and orange stripes caused by alternating organic, and clay and silica, surface layers.

# SOUTH-WEST KIMBERLEY

# FROM CROSSING TO COAST

Stretching from the rugged ranges of the central Kimberley to the edge of the Great Sandy Desert, much of the south-west is dominated by the mighty Fitzroy River. The river hits the Kimberley coast just south of Derby after slicing its way through spectacular gorges on Mornington station and ancient limestone reef ranges above Fitzroy Crossing. Its vast catchment area means it is subject to enormous floods in the Wet, often rising over 15 metres in beautiful Geikie Gorge. West of Derby, the Dampier Land peninsula offers endless sparkling beaches and stunningly weathered coastal cliffs.

An alternate route between the Great Northern Highway west of Fitzroy Crossing and the Gibb River Road provides access to two of the south-west's most spectacular features. Now protected as national parks, towering Windjana Gorge on the Lennard River and the subterranean Tunnel Creek are also connected with the turbulent early history of the region.

The area around the nearby town of Derby was the first section of the Kimberley to feel the encroachment of European settlement. In the early 1890s, after Halls Creek began to prosper during the gold rush, pastoralists began to squeeze Aborigines from their land. As areas once rich in bush food were swamped with sheep and cattle, local Aboriginal people became less tolerant of the newcomers.

In 1894 two police stations were established in the region: one at the present site of Fitzroy Crossing and the other at Lillimilura station near Windjana Gorge.

**PREVIOUS PAGES:** Sunset at Cape Leveque on the northern-most tip of the Dampier Land peninsula makes the weathered cliffs behind the beach glow like hot coals.

That same year, a police tracker named Pigeon, or Jandamarra, began his war against the invasion of white settlers. In a sudden change of sides, he killed Constable Richardson after they had rounded up 15 local Bunaba people at Lillimilura. This led to the legendary Battle of Windjana Gorge where Pigeon and some of his comrades were wounded. After several years of daring cattle raids and evading police patrols,

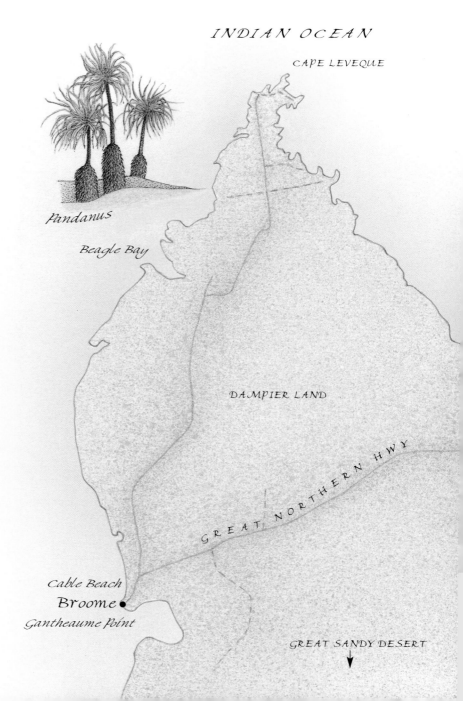

INDIAN OCEAN

CAPE LEVEQUE

Pandanus

Beagle Bay

DAMPIER LAND

GREAT NORTHERN HWY

Cable Beach
Broome •
Gantheaume Point

GREAT SANDY DESERT

Pigeon was betrayed and in April 1897 he was cornered and ultimately shot after a fierce gun battle. Today, a Pigeon Heritage Trail includes the boab 'Prison Tree' near Derby, Windjana Gorge, Tunnel Creek and the Lillimilura Police Station ruins.

After heat-filled days exploring Fitzroy Crossing and the rugged lower gorge country, Broome—with its huge sweeping beach, cosmopolitan lifestyle and rich history—seems like an oasis of comfort and civilisation. This thriving tourist town of camel rides and crocodile farms has also been one of the world's most important pearling centres since the 1890s. Originally based on mother-of-pearl, the industry—once sustained by Aboriginal and Malay divers—was saved from the post-World War II plastic invasion by the advent of cultured pearl technology.

North of Broome, on the vast Dampier Land peninsula, kilometres of pristine beaches, isolated bays and the red semi-arid pindan country are waiting to be explored. Beagle Bay, an Aboriginal community about 120 kilometres north of Broome, has a gorgeous church built in 1890 with an ornate mother-of-pearl altar. At the tip of the peninsula, about 200 kilometres from Broome on a reasonable dirt road, Cape Leveque boasts one of the most beautiful parts of the entire Kimberley coastline. The sculptured sandstone cliffs form wild shapes against the bright blue sky and the sand is as white as can be imagined.

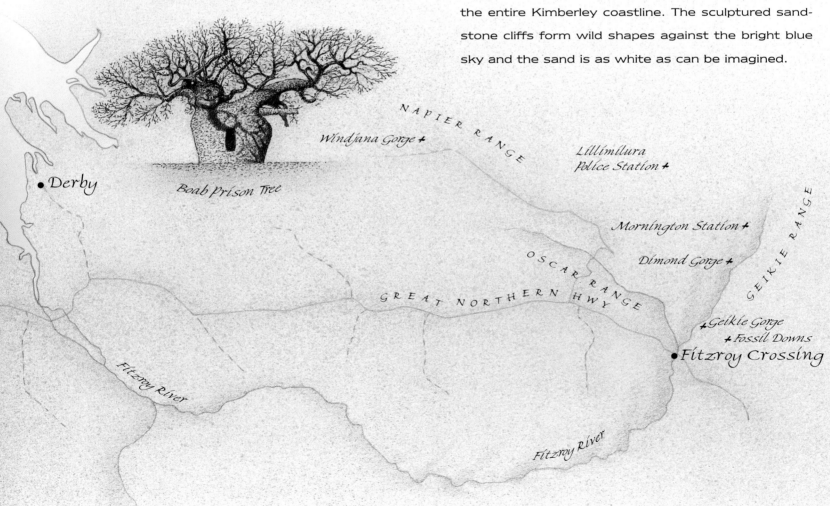

Derby

Boab Prison Tree

Windjana Gorge

NAPIER RANGE

Lillimilura Police Station

Mornington Station

OSCAR RANGE

Dimond Gorge

GEIKIE RANGE

GREAT NORTHERN HWY

Geikie Gorge

Fossil Downs

Fitzroy Crossing

Fitzroy River

Fitzroy River

**RIGHT:** A golden dusk transforms this tumbled rocky ridge near Fitzroy Crossing in the southern Kimberley into a brilliant band of colour beneath a clear blue sky. In the foreground a soft pink Salmon Gum (*Eucalyptus salmonophloia*), typical of the region, catches the last rays of the evening light.

**ABOVE:** The limestone walls of Geikie Gorge, where the mighty Fitzroy River passes through the Geikie Range north of Fitzroy Crossing, were once part of a huge coral reef surrounding what is now the Mitchell Plateau. The pale band at the base of the walls marks the height of the floodline in the Wet.

**RIGHT:** Tunnel Creek, south-east of Windjana Gorge on the track back to the Great Northern Highway, has cut through the lime-stone of Napier Range to form a dramatic underground passage. When the water is low it is possible to explore the full length of the 750-metre tunnel.

**CLOCKWISE FROM TOP LEFT:** The fringed lily (*Thysanotus multiflorus*) is found throughout Western Australia; two tawny frog-mouthed owls (*Podargus strigoides*) pose as broken branches when alarmed; mulla mullas (*Gomphrena canescens*) or bachelor's buttons create a sea of pink after a good Wet; small rock lizards are common all over the Kimberley. **OPPOSITE:** A silvery boab catches the light near Windjana Gorge.

ABOVE: The Lennard River cuts its way through the soft limestone of the Napier Range at Windjana Gorge—the largest and most spectacular gorge in the region. With fluted walls towering up to 100 metres over the sandy floor, Windjana often echoes with the screeches of sulphur-crested cockatoos.

**ABOVE:** Upstream from Geikie Gorge, the Fitzroy River passes through a series of gorges on Mornington Station. Dimond Gorge, one of the most picturesque, is only accessible via a long rough track but the trip is well worth it when you find you have this marvellous place all to yourself.

**ABOVE:** An incredible expanse of perfect white sand meets aqua-blue water at Cable Beach near Broome. Too vast to ever be crowded, the beach is a popular spot for strolls through the sea mists of early morning, frolics in the surf, camel rides and evening barbecues as the sun sets over the Indian Ocean.

**RIGHT:** As the peaceful purple shadows of late evening lengthen, a string of camels and their riders make their way across Cable Beach near Broome on the Indian Ocean. The beach was named for the international telegraph cable to England which came ashore here from Java. The link was finally completed in 1889.

**ABOVE:** The Sacred Heart Church of the small community of Beagle Bay north of Broome was built by monks in 1890 and boasts an altar made of beautifully crafted mother-of-pearl and cowrie shells.

**OPPOSITE:** Traditional pearling luggers have been superseded by fast, modern pearling fleets. Instead of collecting shells at Kuri Bay for pearl farms near Broome, they collect passengers for sunset cruises.

ABOVE: An isolated stand of the strangely shaped pandanus grows on a sand dune at Cape Leveque on the tip of the Dampier Land peninsula. The beaches near this tiny settlement are amongst the few to offer safe swimming this far north, although it is always wise to check with locals wherever you are.

# Photographic Notes

Some people are surprised when I tell them the most important element in photography is 'being there'. Cameras themselves play only a small part in the process because any decent camera should be able to capture great images when the light is right. However, since I go to considerable lengths to be in the right place at the right time, it is a good idea to use the best gear available, thus ensuring that the images I bring back are technically as good as possible. A camera cannot transform a mediocre scene into a great image, but it can certainly create a mediocre image from a superb setting.

For scenic work I like to use medium format as much as possible—the large image area reproduces much better in print. Also, heavier equipment means slower handling. This tends to focus the mind and make for more thoughtful compositions than the first-shot-that-comes-into-your-head that is often the result when using 35 mm.

I use a multi-format Silvestri camera that will shoot 6 x 9 as well as 6 x 12. It has a rotating back and a front perspective shift mechanism which is really useful for controlling converging verticals. Lenses are Schneider 58 mm, 100 mm, 150 mm and 240 mm. The whole lot fits neatly into a Phototreker backpack. The camera always sits on a medium Gitzo tripod—one of my most essential pieces of equipment.

I do believe 35 mm cameras have their place, especially if the subject is likely to move. Most of the people and wildlife pictures in this book are taken on a pair of Canon EOS5s with 17/4, 24/2.8, 28–70/2.8L, 100/2, 135/2L, 300/4L and 400/2.8L Canon lenses.

I use the occasional filter, mostly for contrast control in capturing detail in the sky.

All the images in this book were taken on Fuji Velvia rollfilm or Fuji Provia 35 mm film. No other films capture the colours of the outback in the same way.

Reliable equipment is vital and care must be taken to protect gear from damage. Good storage cases keep out dust and even help with unexpected dunkings. My Phototreker backpack kept my gear mostly dry during an unscheduled swim in Bell Creek, and my orange Pelican cases saved the day during another accidental dip in Lawn Hill Creek. A few hundred dollars invested in good cases is far more practical than insurance in such remote areas, where damage is more likely than theft, but I still have my gear fully insured just in case.

Possibly the most important photographic accessory of all in the Kimberley is a trusty Landcruiser. While there are many good four-wheel-drives on the market, Toyotas seem to be the go in the country so it's not hard to get repairs done.

Finally, safety is a vital aspect of any outback trip, whether you are travelling for work or for pleasure. Over the years I have encountered many poorly prepared visitors who would have been an unnecessary burden on emergency services if trouble had occurred. Plenty of information is available about what precautions to take when preparing for an outback trip—please heed this advice. Of all the items in my car the two most important things would have to be water—lots of it—and a high frequency radio so I can contact the Royal Flying Doctor Service.

# INDEX

First published in Australia in 1999 by New Holland Publishers (Australia) Pty Ltd

Sydney • Auckland • London • Cape Town

14 Aquatic Drive Frenchs Forest NSW 2086 Australia

1A/218 Lake Road Northcote Auckland New Zealand

24 Nutford Place London W1H 6DQ United Kingdom

80 McKenzie Street Cape Town 8001 South Africa

National Library of Australia
Cataloguing-in-publication data:
Rains, Nick
The Kimberley: journey through an ancient land

Includes index.
ISBN 1 86436 432 7.

1. Kimblerley (W.A.) - Pictorial works. I. Title

919.414

Publishing General Manager: Jane Hazell
Publisher: Averill Chase
Project Coordinator: Julie Nekich
Editors: Emma Wise and Julie Nekich
Designer: Tricia McCallum
Map Illustrator: Mike Gorman
Reproduction: Hirt and Carter
Printer: Tien Wah Press (Pte.) Ltd